Princess DIANA

I think the biggest disease this world
suffers from in this day and age is the
disease of people feeling unloved. I
know that I can give love for a minute,
for an half an hour, for a day, for a
month . . . and I want to do that.
—*Diana, Princess of Wales*

Princess DIANA

Katherine Krohn

A&E

Lerner Publications Company
Minneapolis

For Mony

A&E and **BIOGRAPHY** are trademarks of the A&E Television Networks, registered in the United States and other countries.

Some of the people profiled in this series have also been featured in A&E's acclaimed BIOGRAPHY series, which is available on videocassette from A&E Home Video. Call 1-800-423-1212 to order.

Lerner Publications Company
241 First Avenue North
Minneapolis, MN 55401

Website address: www.lernerbooks.com

Library of Congress Cataloging-in-Publication Data

Krohn, Katherine E.
   Princess Diana / Katherine E. Krohn.
      p. cm. — (A&E biography)
   Includes bibliographical references and index.
   Summary: A biography of the young woman who married Britain's Prince Charles in 1981 and lived in the public eye until her tragic death in 1997.
   ISBN 0-8225-4941-7 (alk. paper)
   1. Diana, Princess of Wales, 1961–1997—Juvenile literature.
   2. Princesses—Great Britain—Biography—Juvenile literature.
   [1. Diana, Princess of Wales, 1961–1997. 2. Princesses. 3. Women—Biography.] I. Title. II. Series.
   DA591.A45D5328   1999
   941.085'092
   [B]—DC21   98-27491

Manufactured in the United States of America
1 2 3 4 5 6 – JR – 04 03 02 01 00 99

CONTENTS

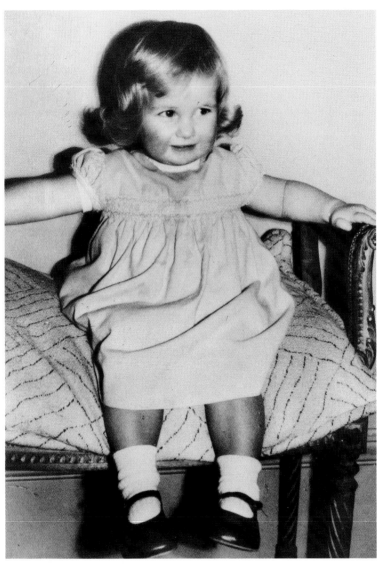

Diana as a toddler sits for photographs at Park House.

Chapter **ONE**

THE GIRL NEXT DOOR

TWELVE-YEAR-OLD **DIANA SPENCER'S SKY BLUE EYES** had a "faraway look." She was daydreaming again. A classmate at West Heath School in Kent, England, had just asked her what she wanted to be when she grew up. "I would love to be a dancer," said Diana. "Or, the Princess of Wales."

Diana wasn't just dreaming. Becoming a princess may have seemed out of reach to most people, but not to her. Diana hailed from one of Great Britain's most noble families. Her ancestors had been special officers of the English royal family and had held official titles. These titles were passed from generation to generation.

One of Diana's ancestors was the first Earl Spencer. In the fifteenth century, he was one of the wealthiest sheep traders in Europe. Earl Spencer bought a vast estate north of London called Althorp. The estate was passed to the next Earl Spencer when the first one died. Diana's grandfather was the seventh Earl Spencer. When he died, Diana's father would inherit the title.

In 1961, Diana Spencer's parents, Edward John "Johnnie" Spencer and Frances Ruth Burke Roche Spencer (known by their official titles as Viscount and Lady Althorp), eagerly awaited the birth of their third child. If the baby were a boy, he too would someday inherit the title of Earl Spencer and all its privileges.

On July 1, 1961, a brilliant summer sun shone over the stately Spencer mansion, Park House, on the huge Sandringham estate in Norfolk in eastern England. The air was hot, and a slight wind carried the scent of purple heather. Late that afternoon, in an upstairs bedroom at Park House, Diana Frances Spencer was born.

At seven pounds twelve ounces, the blonde baby was healthy and strong. Johnnie and Frances loved their new daughter, but, privately, they were disappointed. They had hoped for a son. Diana had two sisters, Sarah, age six, and Jane, age four. If Johnnie and Frances didn't produce a male heir, the lofty title and valuable property would one day go to a male cousin.

Because the Spencers had hoped for a boy, they hadn't even considered a girl's name for the baby. Diana did not have a name until a week after her birth. "I was the girl who was supposed to be a boy," said Diana.

Baby Diana's cream-colored nursery was in a bedroom on the second floor of Park House. Beyond the nursery window, a gravel drive wound through the twenty-thousand-acre estate, highlighting a view of cattle grazing in distant green fields, pretty parks carpeted with flowers, and a thick forest full of animals, such as foxes and rabbits. Horse stables also stood on the impressive estate, as well as a tennis court and staff cottages. Six servants kept the Spencer household running.

Next door to the Spencer's house on the same estate stood a country home belonging to Queen Elizabeth II—the queen of England. Each year, the queen spent a few weeks at her country home.

Downstairs at Park House each morning, a governess, Gertrude "Ally" Allen, taught school to Sarah, Jane, and several neighbor children. A nanny, Judith Parnell, cared for Diana. In the afternoon, when school was over, Sarah and Jane showered baby Diana with attention. They changed her "nappies" (diapers), bathed her, and treated her, as a maid said, "as if she were their own living doll." Each day after lunch, the nanny took Diana for a stroll in a big old-fashioned black pram, a type of baby carriage. Diana's very first memory was of riding in that springy carriage.

In May 1964, Diana's brother, Charles, was born. The family was thrilled. Finally they had a boy, an heir to the title of earl and the Althorp fortune. Immediately,

Charles received the "royal treatment." He was baptized in Westminster Abbey. The queen of England is one of his godmothers.

In 1965, Diana happily joined her sisters at the Park House school. At first, Diana enjoyed cutting, pasting, and drawing. Over the next two years, she learned to read and write. When her sisters played outdoors, Diana liked to tag along. "Diana quite naturally wanted to be part of her elder sisters' fun, and that caused some resentment at first, because the two

Diana's earliest memories were of this carriage.

older girls simply didn't want a child quite younger than they were trying to take part in their games," remembered a Park House nanny.

Diana was especially close to Charles. "She adored her baby brother Charles and treated him just like a doll, in the same way her sisters had treated her," said Ally. "She would dress him in clothes, and undress him and then start again, but he didn't seem to mind too much."

Each night, Diana's mother tucked her in at bedtime. "She would always be there in the evening for cuddles and bedtime stories," said a household servant. But although Johnnie and Frances spent some time with the children, they were very much in the background. Instead, nannies and a governess did most of the child care. "It was a privileged upbringing out of a different age, a distant way of living from your parents," Diana's brother later said.

Like most children of aristocratic families, Diana was taught discipline, poise, and manners. She learned how to act in social situations. Naughty behavior, especially in public, was forbidden. And she learned that her emotions should always be controlled and kept private. But at age six, Diana was about to learn that some things in life were simply out of her control.

For a short time, Diana lived with her mother in London.

Chapter **TWO**

UPROOTED

IN **1967,** SIX-YEAR-OLD **D**IANA SAT ON THE WOODEN
staircase and clutched the white iron bannister. She
was scared. Her parents had been yelling at each
other. Something was terribly wrong.

Her father had a sad and serious look on his face.
Without saying a word, he carried her mother's suit-
cases out of the house and threw them into the trunk
of the car. Diana listened. She could hear her mother's
feet hurrying across the gravel drive. A car door
slammed. The motor raced, and her mother sped away.

Diana's mother had left Park House forever. She had
grown very unhappy in her marriage and wanted to
start a new life for herself in London. Diana was too
young to understand why her mother was leaving. She

wondered if she had done something wrong that had made her mother go away. Frances assured Diana that she would be back to get her and Charles as soon as she settled into her new apartment in London. Weeks would pass before Frances finally sent for the children.

Three-year-old Charles took the separation from his mother especially hard. At night, Diana could hear her baby brother crying out for his mother. Not knowing what to do, she would bury her head under her pillow and cry too. "I just couldn't bear it," Diana later said. "I could never pluck up enough courage to get out of bed. I remember it to this day."

Diana's sisters had also left home—they had recently gone away to boarding school. With her sisters and mother gone, Park House seemed very empty. Diana was glad when her mother took her, Charles, and their nanny to London a few weeks later.

There, Diana started classes at a girls' day school, and Charles started kindergarten. They spent weekends with their father at Park House. But this arrangement lasted only a short time. Diana's father sought custody of his children. For the next several months, the children were caught in the middle of a bitter court battle.

Many custody battles favor the mother. But, in this case, Johnnie had special ammunition. His wife had been having an affair with wealthy businessman Peter Shand Kydd for several months while she was still married. The courts frowned on this behavior. In June

1968, Johnnie won custody of his children, and Diana and Charles returned to Park House.

Diana felt confused and sad. She also felt lonely. "Daddy never spoke to us about it," she said. "We could never ask questions. [There were] too many nannies. The whole thing was very unstable."

Johnnie did whatever he could to lift his children's spirits and take their minds off problems at home. He built a heated swimming pool in the yard, with a slide and diving board. At night, a revolving underwater light flashed colors through the water. The spectacular Spencer pool was the only one on the Sandringham estate and attracted many of the neighboring children, including the queen's youngest sons, Princes Andrew and Edward.

Shortly after Diana and Charles moved in with their mother, Frances Spencer, pictured here in 1996, lost custody of them both.

Diana kept a whole menagerie of stuffed animals in her room. She also had real pets—an orange tabby cat named Marmalade and a guinea pig named Peanuts. Her family had a pony, Romany, and a springer spaniel, Jill.

Johnnie enrolled Diana and her brother in a small day school, the Silfield School, in King's Lynn. The new school required that all students wear a uniform. Each day Diana wore a red sweater, a gray skirt, and tights.

Though Diana missed her governess, Ally, she liked the new school and enjoyed making new friends. The headmistress at Silfield, Jean Lowe, once gave Diana a commendation for helpfulness. She remembers how kind Diana was to the younger children at the school.

Diana's best friends were Alexandra Lloyd and Penelope Ashton. The two girls both lived near Diana on the Sandringham estate. But while Diana had plenty of friends, she still felt different from the other children. "She was the only girl I knew whose parents were divorced," says former Silfield student Delissa Needham. "Those things just didn't happen then."

When school let out at 3:30 P.M., Diana and her brother would hurry home for tea, sandwiches, cookies, and cakes. After tea, Diana usually played in her nursery or watched television.

On holiday (school vacation), Diana and her brother took the train to London to visit their mother. In April 1969, Frances and Johnnie were officially divorced. A month later, Diana's mother married Peter Shand Kydd.

At age nine, Diana faced another separation. This time, she was the one moving—to Riddlesworth Hall, a boarding school where she would both live and study. She sadly waved good-bye as she watched her father slowly drive away. She held Peanuts in a small cage. At her feet stood a sturdy steel trunk labeled "D. F. Spencer."

Johnnie also felt sad, but he thought he was doing the right thing. He thought the school would give Diana a sense of family. She would be surrounded by children her age, and her teachers would look after her and guide her like a mother would. In England, well-to-do families commonly sent their children to boarding schools.

Riddlesworth Hall was a large sandstone mansion in the countryside, about a two-hour drive from Park House. The school was run by a strict but kind woman, Elizabeth Ridsdale. Each morning, "Riddy" rang an old cowbell, a wake-up call for the 120 girls at the school.

Diana knew that she was expected to be on time and obedient, so when she heard the bell, she quickly got out of bed and put on her uniform—a gray pleated skirt, white shirt, gray knee socks, and heavy black shoes. When she was dressed, Diana stood in line with the other girls to have her hair combed and put in pony tails or braids. At 8:00 A.M., breakfast was served. Then the girls made their beds, said their prayers, and went to class. In addition to her academic schoolwork, Diana studied Scottish dancing and ballet.

Diana plays croquet while on holiday.

Diana's favorite place at school was called Pets' Corner, a little city of animal cages set under evergreen trees on a path called Ghost Walk. The cages held the girls' pets—hamsters, rabbits, mice, and guinea pigs, including Peanuts. Diana kept his cage spotless. When time allowed, she would pet him and let him run around on the school lawn. Diana insisted that the other girls take good care of their pets too. Late in the year, Diana won a prize—the Palmer Cup for Pets' Corner—because she kept Peanuts so healthy and well groomed.

Diana wrote weekly letters to "Mummy and Daddy," as she called her parents. She usually included a drawing as a gift to them. Always, Diana asked her parents to mail her favorite treats, like Twiglets (a kind of cookie), ginger cookies, chocolate cake, and chocolate cream eggs.

On holiday, Diana and her sisters and brother either visited their father at Park House or their mother at her new home on an island off Scotland—a big, comfortable old farmhouse on a windy hill. The children liked the house in Scotland. There, they had Shetland ponies to ride and a beach to explore. Sometimes, Diana's new stepfather took her fishing or showed her how to catch lobsters by leaving traps in the ocean.

Diana never lacked for possessions. Her parents were wealthy enough to give her just about anything she wanted. But even though Diana had a fancy home, servants, and all the toys and nice clothes she wanted, she wasn't very happy. She was shy and withdrawn. She longed for a secure home life, not just material things.

At times, Diana felt like her parents were competing for her affection. When Diana was nine, she was invited to a cousin's wedding. Her mother bought her a pretty green dress for the occasion. Her father gave her an equally nice blue dress. "I can't remember to this day which one I wore but I remember being totally traumatized by [choosing] because it would show favoritism," Diana said.

At age twelve, Diana joined her sisters at a girls' boarding school called West Heath, in Kent, England. Their mother had also attended the school. The headmistress at West Heath, Ruth Rudge, required each girl to do community work. Each week, Diana visited an elderly woman in the nearby town of Seven Oaks. Diana helped the woman in little ways, sometimes grocery shopping and doing light housework. Diana later took on other community service projects.

She discovered that she not only enjoyed helping others but she was also good at it. "I remember she spent many hours caring for the handicapped children at a center near the school," said Rudge. "She was a girl who noticed what needed to be done, then did it willingly and happily. But," Rudge added, "Diana was no goody-goody. She could be naughty—talking when lights went out, hiding her [snacks], and making other

West Heath School

girls giggle at assembly or in class with some timely remarks."

Diana liked to draw and play piano. In school, her favorite subjects were art and dance. Her least favorite subjects were French, math, and needlework. But Diana wasn't very interested in schoolwork. "It wasn't that she was stupid. Anyone who knows Diana knows how quickwitted she [was]," said a schoolmate.

Rather than study, Diana preferred to practice piano, dance, and play outdoors with her friends or her animals. She also liked to read romance novels. She especially enjoyed the books of Barbara Cartland, which usually featured a young woman being "swept off her feet" by a charming and handsome man.

"We . . . used to spend all our time reading . . . really awful romantic slush novels," Diana said. "We read hundreds of them. We had a craze on them. We all used to buy as many as we could in the holidays and sneak them back in, and we'd swap them around."

Romance novels fueled Diana's own daydreams. She tacked a picture of her crush, Prince Charles—the queen's oldest son—over her bed at West Heath. She didn't know the prince, but she hoped to meet him one day.

According to Diana's brother, Charles, Althorp House was a scary place for a child.

Chapter **THREE**

LADY DIANA

ON JUNE 9, 1975, DIANA RECEIVED NEWS THAT her grandfather, Earl Spencer VII, had died. Though she hadn't been close to her grandfather, Diana felt sad. She was also a little worried. She knew that her grandfather's death had great significance. Life for the entire Spencer family was about to change.

With her grandfather's death, Diana's father became the new Earl Spencer. With this title, he also inherited the family home, Althorp, in Northamptonshire outside London. He planned to move the family there.

When their father became an earl, Diana and her sisters also received titles. They became Lady Sarah, Lady Jane, and Lady Diana. Charles, only eleven years old, became the new Viscount Althorp. Diana and her brother and sisters didn't really care about their titles. And they didn't want to leave Park House. They hated Althorp, which they had visited only a few times. "It was like an old man's club with masses of clocks ticking away," said Charles. "For an impressionable child, it was a nightmarish place."

On moving day, in the summer of 1975, Charles sadly said good-bye to every room in Park House. Diana was too upset to stay at home and watch the movers carry things out of the house. Instead, she called up her best friend, Alexandra Lloyd. Diana and Alexandra spent one last day at the nearby beach, eating peaches and swimming in the sea.

Althorp was a five-hundred-year-old mansion in the English countryside. In a way, the house was more like a museum than a home. Portraits of long-dead relatives and other valuable artwork (one of the largest collections in England) decorated the walls. The shelves were covered with fine porcelain and rare books. There was no swimming pool, no horses, and no nearby ocean. Diana missed Park House.

Diana tried to make the best of the new situation, though she never considered Althorp to be her home. Soon after the move, Johnnie remarried. His new wife was Raine, the Countess of Dartmouth. Interestingly, Raine was the daughter of Diana's favorite author, Barbara Cartland. Neither Diana nor her siblings liked their stepmother very much. Raine insisted that her servants call her "Countess." She only spoke to her

Raine was Lady Lewisham before she married Diana's father.

household staff to give them orders. Raine always wore an evening gown to dinner, and she insisted that Diana's father wear a tuxedo.

Diana, on the other hand, liked to chat with the servants. She was friendly to everyone, regardless of their rank in the household. Instead of telling servants to do all her chores, Diana did them herself. She did her own washing and ironing when she stayed at Althorp. She also did Charles's laundry.

Diana had lots of energy, and she was an excellent athlete. Eventually, Johnnie had a swimming pool built at Althorp. In the new pool, Diana perfected her "Spencer Special," a dive that barely made any splash or waves in the water. Besides swimming, Diana liked to play net ball (basketball) and tennis.

More than anything, she loved to dance. She set up a record player in the elegant entryway to Althorp. The floor was made of shiny black-and-white marble, and Diana found the surface to be perfect for tap dancing. When she danced, her problems drifted away. She felt graceful and confident.

In June 1977, Diana took her O Level (Ordinary Level) exams, a test British high school students must pass before they further their studies. To her great disappointment, she didn't pass the test. She would have to take the exam again if she wanted to go further in school.

That same summer, Diana's sister Sarah had big news. She had met Charles, the Prince of Wales, at a horse race, and he had asked her on a date. Prince Charles Philip Arthur George was a champion polo player and an airplane pilot. He had been a commander in the Royal Navy. He had sky dived, climbed mountains, and traveled all over the world. Charles was also the heir to the British throne. Most likely, he would be the next king of England. And he was unmarried. In fact, he was considered the most eligible bachelor in the world.

For the next nine months, Sarah Spencer dated Prince Charles. Photographers followed the pair everywhere they went. The press thought that twenty-eight-year-old Charles might have finally chosen a bride. But, gradually, the romance turned into a friendship. Diana was somewhat relieved. She liked the prince too.

In November 1977, Sarah invited Prince Charles to Althorp for a foxhunt. She asked Diana to join the party. Finally, Diana would meet the prince. On the day of the hunt, Diana stood and watched Prince Charles and the other men. In Great Britain, especially among aristocrats, fox hunting is a traditional sport. Typically, the men and boys do the shooting. They are called the "guns." The women and girls stand back and watch the guns hunt.

In a plowed field called Wobottle Wood, Sarah arranged a meeting between Diana and Prince Charles. Diana curtsied, then shyly shook his hand. She thought the quiet and reserved prince was even more handsome in person than in the photograph over her bed at West Heath. The picture didn't capture his charm, energy, or confidence.

Though Diana was excited to meet Prince Charles, she was very careful to use correct etiquette. She only addressed the prince as "Sir." To call him anything else would have been improper. Even Diana's sister, a close friend to the prince, always called him "Sir."

Charles liked Diana, but he didn't yet have romantic feelings for her. "What a very jolly and amusing and attractive sixteen-year-old," he thought. "I mean great fun—bouncy and full of life and everything."

After the hunt, lunch was served at Althorp. Diana, Sarah, Prince Charles, and other friends dined on a hot stew with mashed potatoes and brussels sprouts— a traditional English meal. For dessert, they ate the prince's favorite treat, treacle sponge, a cake made with molasses.

Back at West Heath, Diana found it hard to concentrate on her studies. Her thoughts often turned to Prince Charles. She wondered when she would see him again.

In December 1977, Diana took her O Levels again. For the second time, she failed the test. Discouraged, sixteen-year-old Diana didn't want to return to West Heath. She didn't dare take, and fail, her exams again. She wasn't sure what to do with herself.

Her parents had an idea. Diana's sister Sarah had attended a finishing school—a private school for girls that emphasized culture and social activities. The school, Institut Alpin Videmanette in Switzerland, was very expensive. But students didn't need high test

Gstaad, home of the Institut Alpin Videmanette

scores to attend. Diana's parents thought she would benefit from studying abroad. At finishing school, she would meet girls from all over the world. But Diana had never been out of England. She had never flown on an airplane.

In January 1978, Diana left for Switzerland and joined the school at midterm. There, she studied dressmaking and French. In fact, the school required students to speak French at all times, and of the sixty pupils, only nine spoke English. Diana, who preferred to speak English, made one lasting friend at the school, another British girl, Sophie Kimball.

As the Spencers had hoped, Diana blossomed at the school. Daily ski trips and new friends lifted her spirits and boosted her confidence. "Diana wasn't a scrap shy at all. In fact, she was great fun to be with," said Sophie Kimball.

A few months later, at the end of the term, Diana headed back to England. She wasn't sure what to do with herself next. But she was ready for something completely new.

Diana was determined to live in London.

Chapter **FOUR**

WORKING
WOMAN

AFTER RETURNING TO ENGLAND, DIANA SEARCHED for direction. She figured she couldn't return to West Heath because she hadn't passed her exams. But she didn't want to return to Althorp, which didn't feel like home. Diana thought she'd like to live on her own. Her sisters now lived in London. So Diana asked her parents if she could get an apartment in London too.

Frances gave Diana a firm no. After all, Diana was only sixteen years old. But Frances had another idea. Why not go to work? Diana had never worked a paying job before.

Frances had some friends, the Whitakers, who needed a mother's helper. Frances thought Diana would be perfect for the job. Diana loved children, and children loved her. The Whitakers agreed to hire Diana. They were delighted to have a noblewoman caring for their child. For three months, Diana lived with the Whitakers in Hampshire and worked as a nanny to six-year-old Alexandra.

When Diana's assignment with the Whitakers ended, she again pleaded with her parents to let her live in London. Finally, Frances compromised. She suggested that Diana move into an apartment she owned, at Cadogan Place in an area of London called Chelsea. Frances figured that since she visited London often, she could keep an eye on her daughter.

Diana rented out rooms in the apartment to school friends Laura Grieg and Sophie Kimball. As a joke, they referred to themselves as "Sloane Rangers," the nickname for wealthy young women in Chelsea who were thought to be passing time before they married rich men.

But Diana wasn't just passing time. Although her parents were wealthy and she didn't lack for money, Diana wanted to pay her own bills. For a while, she worked as a waitress for a catering company. She also worked as a house cleaner. Though she was a noble-woman, Diana didn't mind physical labor at all.

Diana also looked for more child-care work. She applied at several temporary employment agencies in London and was sent on a few short-term assignments.

In the fall of 1978, Diana enrolled in a gourmet cooking course. For three months, Diana perfected her cooking skills. She made sauces, omelettes, and soufflés. Her specialties were Russian beet borscht and chocolate roulades.

While Diana was in the cooking class, she received bad news. Her father had suffered a severe stroke. He wasn't expected to live. But, over the next several months, Diana's father slowly regained his health.

In January 1979, the queen invited Diana and Sarah to another hunting party, this one at the Sandringham estate. Diana was excited when she received her invitation. She knew that Prince Charles would be there.

Prince Charles was one of the best gunmen in Great Britain, and he took fox hunting very seriously. At the party, he was so engrossed in hunting that he barely spoke to Diana at all. Disappointed, Diana assumed that Prince Charles was ignoring her and that he did not like her. So she was very surprised to receive a phone call from Charles a few days after the party. He asked her to accompany him and some friends on a trip to the ballet. Diana gladly accepted the invitation and went with the group, though she wished she could spend some time alone with Charles.

Later that summer Diana gave herself a very special gift for her eighteenth birthday. With money that she had inherited from her grandmother, Diana bought her own flat (apartment) in London, at 60 Coleherne Court. She rented rooms to three of her school friends, Virginia Pitman, Carolyn Pride, and Anne Bolton.

Diana had fun fixing up her new place. She painted the living room pale primrose yellow. She wanted a cheery bathroom, so she painted the walls with bold colors, topped off with bright red cherries.

Diana's roommates often saw her scurrying around the apartment with her rubber gloves on, scrubbing and cleaning. She was proud of her home and liked to keep it tidy. Because she was the landlord, she got the biggest bedroom in the flat. As a joke, she hung a sign on her bedroom door that read "Chief Chick."

She liked to watch TV with her roommates, read, shop, and meet friends at the local bistro for lunch. Sometimes, the roommates threw dinner parties. "We did have a great time together," said Carolyn Pride. "It was fun, with lots of laughter and silliness. . . . We were young and learning to enjoy life. But there was nothing wild about any of us."

Diana had boyfriends, but she didn't get very serious with any of them. Occasionally, she went out with Prince Charles, but the relationship remained casual. Diana hoped it would grow into a romance.

In the fall of 1979, Diana began working at the Young England Kindergarten in the Pimlico district of London. Three days a week, she rode her bicycle the short distance to the school. There, she supervised art class for fifty toddlers. She mixed paints, washed brushes, and looked after them while they worked. Just a few months later, Diana took on a second job. For the two other days each week, she baby-sat for Patrick Robertson, the child of an American family who was living in London at the time.

Despite her busy schedule, Diana always made time for dancing—though at five feet ten inches, she had grown too tall to dance professionally. She wanted to teach dancing, so she enrolled in a teaching course at the Betty Vancini Dance School in the Knightsbridge area of London. The program was intensive. Students were required to study for three years and practice dancing several hours each day.

Shortly after enrolling in the school, Diana joined her friend Mary Ann Stewart-Richardson for a short skiing trip in the French Alps. On one ski run, Diana

Diana poses with two of her students at the Young England Kindergarten.

fell and tore all of the tendons in her left ankle. She didn't let her injury get her down, though. She couldn't continue her studies at dance school, but she still managed to work and socialize with friends. Prince Charles helped brighten Diana's spirits too. Over the next few months, he asked her out several times.

Sometimes Diana didn't hear from Prince Charles for a month or two. When they did go out, they were never alone. Diana had strong feelings for the prince. She wished he would see her as more than a friend.

In May 1980, Diana's sister Sarah got married to Neil McCorquodale. Diana acted as the chief bridesmaid for her sister. She even caught the bridal bouquet. Two years earlier, Diana's sister Jane had married Robert Fellowes. Diana wondered when she would marry. Her thoughts often turned to Prince Charles.

The prince himself was under a lot of pressure. His mother, Queen Elizabeth, and his father, Prince Philip, wanted him to choose a wife. As their oldest son, Prince Charles would one day be crowned the king of England. He was expected to marry and produce a male heir to the throne.

The press also pressured the prince. Photographers followed him wherever he went. Often, newspapers showed him with a girlfriend. The public also wanted to know—when was the prince going to settle down and get married?

For Prince Charles, choosing a bride was an almost agonizing decision. He had been in several promising relationships. But none of the romances had lasted. He still had feelings for one old girlfriend, Camilla Parker-Bowles, but she had married someone else.

Prince Charles wanted to make the right choice. His bride had to come from an upstanding, aristocratic family. She had to be comfortable among royalty and understand royal traditions. As a member of the royal family, she would have to make public appearances and host charity benefits.

"When you marry in my position you are going to marry someone who perhaps one day is going to be queen," Prince Charles told a reporter. "You have to choose somebody very carefully, I think, who could fill this particular role."

With the encouragement of his father and mother, the thirty-two-year-old prince edged closer to a decision.

Prince Charles with his dog Harvey at Balmoral

Chapter **FIVE**

OLD-FASHIONED COURTSHIP

DIANA'S HEART WAS POUNDING. SHE WAS SMILING from ear to ear. "Quick," she yelled to her roommate Carolyn. "I've got to meet Charles in twenty minutes!"

Diana and Carolyn giggled as they frantically ransacked Diana's closet. Diana had a spur-of-the-moment date with the Prince of Wales. "We had the funniest time ever, getting the hair washed, getting it dried, getting the dress—where's the dress. We did it in twenty minutes flat," remembered Carolyn.

Just a few weeks earlier, in July 1980, Diana's friendship with the prince had finally bloomed into a romance. Prince Charles had invited Diana to watch him play polo with his team. Afterward, Diana joined the prince and the others for an outdoor barbecue.

At last, seated next to Prince Charles on a bale of hay, Diana had some private time to talk to him. She had seen him at the funeral of Lord Mountbatten, who had been slain by Irish terrorists. Though he was Prince Charles's uncle, Lord Mountbatten had been like a father to him.

"You looked so sad when you walked up the aisle at the funeral," Diana said to Prince Charles. "My heart bled for you. . . . I thought, it's wrong, you are lonely, you should be with somebody to look after you."

Prince Charles was touched by Diana's words. She seemed to understand him in a way no one else did. He didn't know why or when exactly, but his feelings for Diana had grown stronger. He wanted to see her again soon.

Later that month, Prince Charles invited Diana on a trip aboard the royal yacht *Britannia,* moored off the Isle of Wight. Her childhood friends, Prince Charles's brothers, Andrew and Edward, were also onboard.

Diana was excited to be aboard the famous vessel. She enjoyed exploring the yacht and meeting the crew. "The crew of the *Britannia* fell in love with her . . . the Royal servants liked her," recalled the prince's valet, Stephen Barry. "The stewards ran around saying, 'Gosh, isn't Lady Di lovely?' . . . We all sensed that here was someone different. Someone who might get 'the job,' as the staff referred to a potential Princess of Wales."

As Prince Charles's feelings for Diana grew, he wanted her to meet others in his family, especially his mother. In September 1980, the queen invited Diana to Balmoral, her home in Scotland, for a deer-hunting weekend. The queen was eager to officially meet Lady Diana, whom she remembered as a child from Park House on the Sandringham estate. Perhaps, the queen hoped, her son had found a serious girlfriend.

Later, Diana spent the night with her sister Jane and Jane's husband, Robert, who worked for the queen and lived in a cottage on the estate. Over the next several days, Prince Charles called Diana at the cottage and asked her to join him for walks and a fishing trip on the River Dee, which snaked through the Balmoral grounds.

While watching Prince Charles fish for salmon, nineteen-year-old Diana had her first encounter with the reporters who constantly stalked the prince. As she stood on the banks of the river, she spied two men with cameras lurking at the top of a hill behind her.

Diana tried to outsmart the photographers. She pulled a small hand mirror from her purse and watched the men edge near. She wrapped a scarf around her head and put on a flat cap, disguising her identity, then walked straight up the hill past the men. The reporters snapped her picture, but they couldn't tell who she was.

Diana's photograph—in her disguise—ran Monday, September 8, 1980, in newspapers all over the world. Despite Diana's attempts to stay anonymous, the press had discovered her name. Headlines read: "LADY DIANA

SPENCER—PRINCE CHARLES'S NEW GIRLFRIEND" and "HE'S IN LOVE AGAIN."

Diana's private life was officially over. For the next five months, members of the news media camped outside her apartment building. When she left home, reporters surrounded her and asked: "Are you in love with Prince Charles?"

Diana didn't know how to handle the crowd of aggressive reporters. At first, she tried to ignore them while they snapped photographs and bombarded her with questions. But the reporters were persistent. They followed her everywhere.

Sometimes Diana tried to be polite. She often smiled at the reporters and said she that couldn't answer any of their questions. In newspaper photographs, Diana

Diana's father holds tabloid newspapers featuring Diana and Prince Charles.

usually had her head bowed, and she often peered through her bangs. The press nicknamed her "Shy Di."

Journalists also reported that Diana was "chubby" and "plump." The criticism bothered her so much that she immediately went on a diet.

Diana felt overwhelmed. Her life was changing too fast. She could no longer do routine things like ride her bike. She had to drive everywhere. She couldn't go to the grocery store without being followed. Reporters even followed her to her babysitting and kindergarten jobs, disturbing activities at the school.

Diana's boss at the Young England Kindergarten, headmistress Kay King, had a suggestion. "We didn't know how to get rid of the press, so I suggested that if we allowed them to take one photograph, they might go away."

Diana agreed to pose for the photographers, but she didn't want to pose alone. "She was very insistent that she take some of the children with her," added King. "I think she felt safer, as if they were her protection."

The next day, a photograph of Diana posing with two little girls from the kindergarten appeared in the *London Evening Standard*. Diana was shocked when she saw the photo. With the sunlight behind her, her skirt appeared to be see-through. The embarrassing picture soon appeared in hundreds of magazines and newspapers around the world.

Diana was horrified. She had trusted the photographers and they had taken advantage of her. When

Prince Charles saw the photograph, he tried to make Diana laugh. "I knew your legs were good, but I didn't know they were that good," he joked.

Diana tried to adjust to the growing worldwide obsession with her romance. She wanted the relationship to work because by now she had fallen deeply in love. She knew she would put up with anything to be with Prince Charles.

On February 5, 1981, over a romantic dinner and champagne, Prince Charles proposed to Diana. Though the occasion was a happy one, his tone was serious. He warned Diana that if she married him, she would have to say good-bye to her former life. As the Princess of Wales, she would never be able to go anywhere alone again. A police officer would accompany her everywhere. Her privacy would be gone forever.

Prince Charles didn't want an answer from Diana right away. She could give him her answer when she returned from a vacation with her mother in Australia. "I wanted to give her a chance to think about it," Charles said, "to think if it was going to be too awful."

Diana didn't need any extra time to consider Prince Charles's proposal. She knew her answer even before she left for Australia. Two agonizing weeks later, when Diana returned to England, she gave Prince Charles a definite yes.

Diana and Prince Charles tried to keep their engagement a secret for a few days—unsuccessfully. "I saw Diana in her flat, and I guessed when I saw her face.

The royal engagement was announced to the public on February 24, 1981.

She was totally radiant, bouncing and bubbly," remembered Diana's sister Sarah. "I said 'You're engaged,' and she said yes. I was so happy, so thrilled for her, for it was the first time in her life that Diana had felt really secure."

On February 24, 1981, the engagement was officially announced at Buckingham Palace, the London home of the British monarchy. "The atmosphere at the Palace was electric. Everyone from the kitchens to the Household knew that something was up," said valet Stephen Barry. "Cases of pink champagne were being chilled and we felt as if an explosion was about to happen."

The royal household cheered when Lord Chamberlain of the queen's staff made the formal announcement: "It is with the greatest pleasure that Her Majesty, the Queen, and the Duke of Edinburgh [Prince Philip], announce the betrothal of their beloved son, the Prince of Wales, to Lady Diana, daughter of the Earl Spencer and the Honorable Mrs. Shand Kydd."

Next, officials posted the announcement on the gates of Buckingham Palace. Within an hour, people all over the world knew about the engagement. The following day, Diana and Prince Charles posed for photographers and talked to reporters. Diana showed off her engagement ring, which featured a big blue sapphire surrounded by fourteen diamonds. A wedding date was set, July 29, 1981.

Diana was certain of her feelings for Charles. She was deeply in love and thought that she and the prince made an excellent team. "Diana seemed bowled over by Charles. She worshipped the ground he walked on. She was constantly kissing and touching him, telling him how much she loved him," remembered Stephen Barry. "I had never seen anyone be like this with Charles before. But he seemed to like it."

When an interviewer asked the couple if they were in love, Diana replied, "Of course." But the prince didn't answer the question directly. "Whatever love is," he added.

Soon after the engagement was announced, Diana moved into Buckingham Palace to prepare for a royal life and her July wedding. The secluded environment of the palace also gave Diana some much needed privacy and protection from reporters.

Diana was going to miss her friends and the ordinary, casual lifestyle they had shared. She also sensed that her days ahead weren't going to be easy. On the day she moved out of her London flat, Diana left her roommates a note. Along with her new phone number, she said, "For God's sake ring me up—I'm going to need you."

Prince Charles was often out of town on official duties, so Diana kept in touch with him by telephone. The two had long telephone talks almost every evening.

Sometimes, Diana met her friends for lunch in the city, but a security guard always came along. At home at the palace, Diana practiced ballet or listened to music. She liked Elton John, Dire Straits, and the Beach Boys. She also liked Tchaikovsky.

Though Diana wasn't yet a princess, she was treated like one. She could pick up a phone and ask the palace staff to bring her anything. If she wanted a meal, tea, a bath run, or clothes ironed, a servant would promptly respond.

Diana made a point of personally meeting everybody who worked at the palace, including the maids, the kitchen staff, the secretaries, and the receptionists. "No member of the Royal Family had ever taken the trouble to meet and talk to the staff on equal terms before," observed a writer. "Naturally, Diana's action won her the eternal devotion of those who worked at Buckingham Palace."

Diana and Charles planned to move into the prince's country home, Highgrove, after their marriage. Diana had fun working with an interior decorator to turn Prince Charles's "getaway" into a comfortable home. But before they could even begin decorating, security measures were needed. Workmen knocked down several walls in the house to create a steel-walled inner room. The steel wall would shield the royal couple in case of a terrorist attack. Bulletproof glass was placed in all the windows.

As a wedding gift, the couple would also receive an apartment in Kensington Palace, the seventeenth-century London home of King William III and Queen Mary II, which had been converted by King George III into royal apartments. Diana's sister Jane and her husband also lived at Kensington Palace.

Besides decorating her two new homes, Diana prepared for her wedding day. She met with David and Elizabeth Emanuel, a husband-and-wife design team who would create a very special wedding dress. The bridal train was going to be extremely long—twenty-five feet. Diana didn't want to trip on the train on her wedding day, so she practiced her walk up the aisle by dragging two bed sheets tied together around the palace ballroom.

Diana's sister Jane had worked as an editorial assistant at *Vogue* magazine in London. Jane called her friends at the magazine and set up a fashion consultation for Diana. Although Diana had always been a stylish dresser, the *Vogue* staff worked with Diana to choose a distinctive new look. She let go of the button-down sweaters and light cotton skirts of her teenage years. She incorporated frilly high-necked blouses, brightly colored tailored suits, stylish hats, and designer evening gowns into her wardrobe. A former model who worked at *Vogue*, Grace Coddington, gave Diana some pointers on how to act in front of the cameras—how to stand, sit, smile, and walk gracefully.

In addition, Diana's longtime hairdresser, Kevin Stanley of Headlines salon in London, gave her thick blonde hair a short, elegant cut. Soon, women all over the globe would copy the "Lady Diana Haircut."

Within a few weeks, Diana's self-assurance grew. She faced photographers, reporters, TV cameras, and her fans with growing confidence. She also became more comfortable talking to reporters. The news media as well as the public seemed to adore her. Diana was ready for her new life. The royal wedding was just around the corner.

Millions of people watched the royal wedding.

Chapter **SIX**

THE WEDDING OF THE CENTURY

IN THE SUMMER OF **1981,** ENGLAND WAS IN A state of distress. An economic recession had spread across the country. Angry race riots rocked the streets of London. Meanwhile, discord echoed around the world. In Rome, a gunman attempted to kill Pope John Paul II. In the United States, President Ronald Reagan was shot in an attempted assassination.

With so much gloom in the air, spirits needed lifting. People all over the world needed something to feel good about. They needed fantasy, an escape. The wedding of Lady Diana and Prince Charles came at the right time.

On July 29, 1981, Diana awoke at 6:30 A.M. to the sound of many voices. Outside her bedroom window, thousands of people filled the streets, eagerly awaiting the royal procession from Buckingham Palace to Saint Paul's Cathedral, where Diana and Charles would wed. Diana could hardly believe it. Was she dreaming? She couldn't believe that so many people had come to see *her* get married.

When Diana's hair and makeup were done, Elizabeth Emanuel and her assistants helped Diana slip into her wedding gown. Diana resembled a fairy-tale princess. Her dress was made of crisp, ivory-colored silk, taffeta, and lace, covered with hundreds of tiny sequins and pearls, all sewn on by hand. The hand-embroidered twenty-five-foot long train was the

The train on Diana's wedding gown was the longest in royal history.

longest in British wedding history. "Diana's dress was an absolute expression of how she felt at the time," commented fashion critic Suzy Menkes. "She was very young, very romantic. . . . [The dress] was exactly right to express that moment."

Four horse-drawn carriages took the royal family to Saint Paul's Cathedral. Diana rode in an antique glass carriage escorted by mounted police. Her long train billowed around her like a white cloud, completely filling the coach. Next to Diana sat her father, Earl Spencer.

Diana was in a lighthearted mood. All along the pathway to the church, she and her father made little jokes. Her father pointed out funny signs in the crowd. At one point, Diana suddenly began singing an advertising jingle for an English brand of ice cream, "Just One Cornetto." Laughing helped ease Diana's nerves as her carriage moved past the masses of well-wishers.

When the coach arrived at Saint Paul's Cathedral, Diana stepped onto a red carpet leading into the church. Her five bridesmaids were waiting for her, and they helped spread out her train. Diana took her father's arm and began her walk down the long aisle of the cathedral.

Because of his stroke, walking was difficult for Earl Spencer. When Diana and her father reached the front of the high altar, she clasped her father's right hand. With her left hand, she steadied him. Afterward, Earl Spencer said of Diana, "She was a tower of strength."

Next, Diana joined Prince Charles at the altar. The Archbishop of Canterbury performed the ceremony. Diana and Prince Charles were nervous. Instead of saying "all my worldly goods with thee I share," Prince Charles goofed up and said "all thy goods with thee I share." Diana stumbled over her lines too. She referred to her husband-to-be as "Philip Charles Arthur George" instead of "Charles Philip Arthur George." "She married my father," Prince Charles later joked.

During the ceremony, crowds outside Buckingham Palace listened to the wedding on radios. When the archbishop pronounced Diana and Charles as husband and wife, the crowds cheered. Inside the cathedral, the queen smiled radiantly. The Queen Mother (Queen Elizabeth's mother) wiped away tears of joy.

After posing for wedding photos, the newlyweds rode back to Buckingham Palace in an open carriage, followed by the other royal family members. The crowds cheered and threw rice and confetti.

Once the royal family got back to the palace, the crowd yelled for them to come out on the balcony. After the queen, Queen Mother, and Princes Philip, Edward, Andrew, and Charles appeared, the crowd yelled, "We want Di, we want Di, we want Di."

Diana was overwhelmed. She shyly took Prince Charles's hand and stepped onto the balcony. The crowd yelled, "Kiss her, kiss her." When Prince Charles kissed Princess Diana on the lips, the crowd went wild.

The crowd gets a royal treat from the newlyweds.

"Neither of us will ever forget the atmosphere. It was electric, almost unbelievable," remembers Prince Charles. "I remember standing at my window trying to realize what it was like so that I might be able to tell my own children."

Diana's fairy-tale day ended with a ride aboard the royal train to Broadlands, a sixteenth-century, six-thousand-acre estate that had belonged to Prince Charles's beloved uncle, Lord Mountbatten. There, Diana and the prince spent their wedding night. Prince Charles's parents had also honeymooned at Broadlands. Two days later, Diana and Prince Charles left for a two-week Mediterranean cruise aboard the royal yacht *Britannia*.

On their honeymoon, Charles and Diana pose for photographers.

Chapter **SEVEN**

BABY WALES

WE WANT DIANA! WE WANT DIANA!" YELLED the crowd on a rainy October day in Wales. Three months after their wedding, Princess Diana and Prince Charles visited Wales on their first official "walkabout," a tour to meet the public.

Diana stepped out of a limousine, followed by Prince Charles. "There she is! There she is!" the people cried as Diana came into view. "There she is!"

Thousands craned their heads, trying to get a glimpse or a photo of Diana. People tried to get close enough to shake her hand. Some people handed her flowers.

The prince felt a little uncomfortable. Before the wedding, he had been the focus of attention. Now people seemed to prefer Diana. Prince Charles tried to make the best of the situation. He smiled, shook hands, and apologized to the people who couldn't see his wife. His arms were full of presents from the crowd. Most of the gifts were for Diana.

Though Diana was soaked from the rain, she insisted on shaking as many hands as possible. She was amazed that so many people liked her. But her popularity really wasn't surprising. She was warm and friendly, not formal and serious like most members of the royal family. She was beautiful and charming, but also a little awkward, shy, and vulnerable. These contradictions made people like Diana even more—she seemed like a real person.

Diana was happy when her Welsh tour was over. She had enjoyed her first royal walkabout, but she was tired—for good reason. No one except Prince Charles knew at the time, but Diana was pregnant.

On November 5, 1981, Buckingham Palace officially announced that Diana was pregnant. In the first few weeks of her pregnancy, Diana suffered from morning sickness. She was weak and thin, but she still had royal duties to perform. Diana was expected to make frequent appearances with the prince and, like her husband, perform charity work.

Diana felt an affinity with needy and suffering people. She also felt fulfilled when she visited hospices for the terminally ill. "[When] people are dying, they're much more open and vulnerable, and much more real than other people. And I appreciated that," she said.

When Diana talked to sick people, she listened carefully, and she remembered them. Every meeting was special to her. Diana was very casual. She liked to sit next to patients on their hospital beds and hold their hands. She often greeted patients, especially children, with a kiss on the cheek.

No royal had ever made these kinds of open and intimate gestures toward strangers. Some people, especially those in the royal family, were shocked "because I do things differently, because I don't go by a rule book, because I lead from the heart, not the head," Diana noted.

Diana was often deeply moved by the sad situations she witnessed. She knew that royals were supposed to hide their feelings in public. But when she got home after a long day of touring hospitals, Diana often broke down and cried.

The prospect of motherhood brought Diana joy. She and Prince Charles attended a natural childbirth class together. Nurse Betty Parsons taught Diana breathing techniques that would help her during labor and delivery. Parsons taught Prince Charles and the other men how to be supportive "coaches" for their wives during childbirth.

On June 21, 1982, in a private wing of London's St. Mary's Hospital, Diana gave birth to a boy. Diana and Charles weren't certain what to name the baby. At first they just called him "Baby Wales." He was the first heir to the British throne to have his father present during birth.

The queen was the first person to receive the good news. She and Prince Philip were thrilled, especially because their new grandchild was a boy—an heir to the throne. "Baby Wales" might one day become the king of England. Within minutes, the news was broadcast on TV and radio. The crowds waiting outside the hospital chanted, "It's a boy! It's a boy!" A week later, the baby received his full name, William Arthur Philip Louis. His parents called him, simply, Wills.

Though Diana was happy to have a new baby, after the birth she developed a severe case of depression—not uncommon in new mothers. In Diana's case, the stress of her new and very public life only made the depression worse.

When she woke up in the morning, Diana didn't want to get out of bed. She felt tired and sad. She had never had a serious depression before. "I knew in myself that . . . what I needed was space and time to adapt to all the different roles that had come my way. I knew I could do it, but I needed people to be patient and give me the space to do it."

Prince Charles wasn't sure how to handle Diana's tearful moods. Others in the royal family tried to ignore her depression. Diana really had no choice but to try to pull herself together. She had a child to raise and royal duties to perform. A few months after having the baby, Diana was back to work. But she insisted that her early morning hours be kept free so she could spend as much time as possible with Prince

Prince Charles and Princess Diana with "Baby Wales"

William. In the afternoon, Diana usually toured hospitals and visited people in need.

Despite Diana's internal struggles, people still watched her with admiration. Reporters noticed her flair for fashion. Her sense of style transformed the royal image. "[The public] liked the way she thumbed her nose at the rules, throwing away the starchy white gloves so beloved by the older Royal family," said royal biographer Andrew Morton. Because so many women wanted to copy Diana's style, she pumped new vitality into the British fashion industry.

Diana especially liked hats. "Wearing hats gives me confidence," she said. And, as always, women around the world copied her. The hat industry enjoyed a major surge in business thanks to Diana.

Charles wasn't as stylish as Diana—he preferred country life to life in the city. Some reporters noted

Diana liked to wear hats, and women around the world copied her style.

how different Diana and Charles were and claimed they had nothing in common. "Everything [Charles] liked, Diana didn't like," said a friend of Diana's. "Horses and dogs sort of scared her. She couldn't stand the people he had around him, always hunting and shooting. She liked the lights. She liked fashion and music."

In March 1983, Diana and Charles left Great Britain for their first foreign tour—to Australia and New Zealand. Thousands greeted them wherever they went.

Prince Charles was amazed. He had never seen such a large turnout for a royal appearance.

As in Wales, the crowds showed a preference for Diana. When their car passed a crowd, people who couldn't see Diana sometimes said, "Oh, we're [on] the wrong side, we want to see her. We don't want to see him." Diana felt confused. The tour was going tremendously well, but her husband resented her for her popularity.

As usual, the media focused on the clothes Diana wore during the trip. Many of the outfits from Diana's Australia trip inspired the "Lady Di Look," which came into fashion in the fall of 1983. The look featured brightly colored suits and brimmed hats with bows or feathers.

Diana still had a lot to learn about public life. She knew she had better learn fast. The press and the public seemed to be fascinated with every move she made, and the royal family expected her to be "on" all the time.

Diana was glad when the tour of Australia was over. She returned to England feeling stronger and more mature. "It was . . . a situation where you couldn't indulge in feeling sorry for yourself," said Diana. "You had to either sink or swim—I swam."

Prince Harry's christening

Chapter **EIGHT**

HIGHS AND LOWS

IN EARLY **1984,** DIANA DISCOVERED THAT SHE WAS pregnant again. She was excited. Of all her roles and duties, she enjoyed parenthood the most.

On September 15, 1984, Diana gave birth to another healthy baby boy, Henry Charles Albert David, called Harry. The baby was fair skinned, with a tiny crop of red hair.

Soon after Harry's birth, Diana had to attend to her royal duties—more tours of foreign countries. It was hard for Diana to leave her boys behind when she traveled. But the royals thought it wasn't safe to take the boys abroad. Instead, the young princes remained in Great Britain, in the care of nannies, when Diana and Charles traveled.

In England, Diana kept up her charity work, volunteering for almost one hundred organizations. Usually, she worked with people who were dying or very sick. Sometimes she visited sick children or talked to people about their personal problems. Meanwhile, Diana had plenty of her own problems.

She thought her husband seemed kind of distant. She suspected that Charles was meeting privately with his old flame Camilla Parker-Bowles, but she couldn't prove it, and she didn't want to believe it. Instead, she tried to focus on raising her sons and attending to her many royal duties.

Although the stress of her public life was tremendous, Diana felt like she shouldn't complain. She had wanted to be married to the Prince of Wales, after all. Hadn't she gotten exactly what she had wanted?

Sometimes Diana felt like she couldn't face another reporter, or speak for another charity, or smile for another camera, or act polite at yet another royal dinner party. But she had no choice. Many people were depending on her. "There were times of such confusion and despair that I believed Diana was being driven almost to the point of destruction by the incredible pressures on her," said reporter Richard Kay, a friend of Diana's.

Diana didn't want to disappoint the public. She tried to keep herself together, but she was falling apart. Sometimes Diana even hurt herself. When she was alone, she made small cuts on her arms and legs.

Diana was crying out for help. But few were listening. Prince Charles saw the scratches and cuts on Diana's body. He was very concerned, but he didn't know what to say or do.

Diana also developed bulimia, an eating disorder that can have deadly effects. Four or five times a day, Diana would eat a huge meal. The food comforted her at first. But then she would force herself to throw up all she had eaten. "[Eating is] like having a pair of arms around you, but it's . . . temporary," said Diana. "Then you're disgusted at the bloatedness of your stomach, and then you bring it all up again."

Diana and Camilla Parker-Bowles had known each other since before Charles and Diana married.

"I'd come home feeling pretty empty," she explained. "It would be very difficult to know how to comfort myself, having been comforting lots of other people, so it would be a regular pattern to jump into the fridge."

Though she needed help, Diana felt too ashamed to tell anybody about her eating disorder. She thought people would think she was wasting food.

Diana hid her problems and carried on with her public duties and charity work. In a sense, Diana drew strength and healing from the very people she helped. She often felt loved and supported by the public.

In 1985, Princess Diana and Prince Charles made their first official visit to the United States. First Lady Nancy Reagan planned a dinner party in their honor and invited two of Diana's favorite performers—actor John Travolta and dancer Mikhail Baryshnikov.

Diana was seated next to Baryshnikov at the dinner table. When she asked him for his autograph, he was flabbergasted. Baryshnikov didn't know that Diana was a great fan of the ballet. "As a teenager, I stood in the rain outside the stage door at Covent Garden when you were dancing," explained Diana. "I was such an admirer."

Diana was thrilled to meet John Travolta. After dinner, he asked her to dance. "When they began dancing together, everyone cleared the floor. It was a wonderful, magical moment," remembered Mrs. Reagan.

The prince and princess made another official trip in 1986, this time to Canada for the Canadian Expo. At the time, Diana was seriously bulimic. She hadn't kept any food in her stomach for days. She was very thin and weak. But Diana didn't want to complain.

At one point, Diana was walking around, shaking hands and greeting people, when she began to feel dizzy and sick. Diana knew she couldn't hide her illness any longer. She put her arm around Prince Charles and whispered to him, "Darling, I think I'm about to disappear."

Diana fainted. Royal aids hurried her back to her hotel room. But instead of comforting her, Prince Charles was angry. "[You] could have passed out quietly somewhere else, behind a door," said the prince.

Diana was embarrassed. She was also very sick. She knew that she had a serious problem. "A doctor came and saw me," said Diana. "He didn't know what to say because the issue was too big for him to handle. He just gave me a pill and shut me up."

The tension between Charles and Diana began to increase. As Diana had suspected, Prince Charles had renewed his love affair with Camilla Parker-Bowles. Diana knew of the affair, but "I wasn't in a position to do anything about it," she said.

At a birthday party for Camilla's sister in 1987, Diana got up the nerve to confront Camilla about the affair. "Camilla, I would just like you to know that I know exactly what is going on between you and Charles," she said. "I wasn't born yesterday. . . . Don't treat me like an idiot." Though it was difficult, Diana

Diana shakes hands with an AIDS patient in Brazil.

was glad she had told Camilla how she felt. She was tired of hiding her feelings.

Diana wasn't only competing with Camilla for love and attention. There was a new princess on the scene. In 1986, Charles's brother Prince Andrew had married Sarah Ferguson. "Fergie" seemed to love being a royal. "I couldn't understand it," said Diana. "She was actually enjoying being where she was, whereas I was fighting to survive."

Though the two princesses became friends, at first Diana was jealous of Fergie. The press called her a "breath of fresh air" and "more fun than Diana." Even Charles said, "I wish you would be like Fergie—all jolly. Why are you always so miserable?"

Unhappy though she was, Diana turned her energy to helping others. In the mid-1980s, the first cases of AIDS (Acquired Immunodeficiency Syndrome) were reported. There was a lot of fear surrounding the disease. For instance, many people falsely believed they could get AIDS from casual contact, such as shaking hands. As a result, the public shunned AIDS patients. Many people suffered alone with the disease.

In 1987, Diana kindly shook the hand of an AIDS patient in a London hospital. Photographs of the event were soon printed in newspapers worldwide. "You can shake their hands and give them a hug," she said of people with AIDS. "Heaven knows, they need it."

Diana's gesture has helped change the way society treats people with AIDS. Reporter Judy Wade called Diana's act "The most important thing a royal has done in 200 years."

Sometimes Diana was amazed to see how much power she had. She could make a sick or sad person feel much better just by sitting and talking. All she had to do was show up at a benefit and money was donated. But Diana knew that if she wanted to continue helping others, she needed to help herself first.

Diana often felt overwhelmed by her life in the spotlight.

Chapter **NINE**

QUEEN OF PEOPLE'S HEARTS

IN THE FALL OF **1988,** DIANA RECEIVED A PHONE call that changed her life. Carolyn Bartholomew, a childhood friend, was calling to confront Diana about her eating disorder. Carolyn had known about Diana's illness for a while, and she was seriously concerned about Diana's health. She felt it was time to intervene.

"Have you talked to a doctor?" she asked.

"I can't," said Diana.

"You must," said Carolyn. She was angry. She couldn't stand to see Diana suffer anymore. "I'll give you one hour to ring up your doctor, and if you don't, I'm going to tell the world."

Carolyn's harsh words pushed Diana into action. She made an appointment with a therapist. "[The doctor said], in six months' time you won't recognize your-self," Diana recalled. "If you can keep food down you will change completely."

Diana agreed to visit the therapist once a week. Eventually, she regained her self-esteem, and she stopped hurting herself. "I must say, it's like being born again since then," said Diana. "When my bulimia finished, I felt so much stronger mentally and physi-cally, so I was able to soldier on in the world."

When she was stronger, Diana spoke publicly about eating disorders like bulimia and anorexia, which were just beginning to be discussed. "Many would like to believe that eating disorders are merely an expres-sion of female vanity—not being able to get into a size 10 dress and the consequent frustrations," Diana told a women's group. "Eating disorders, whether it be anorexia or bulimia, show how individuals can turn the nourishment of the body into a painful attack on themselves, and they have at their core a far deeper problem than mere vanity."

Despite their personal problems, Charles and Diana worked together to give their sons a balanced view of life. Charles taught William and Harry the traditional sports and activities that he loved, such as hunting, fishing, and horseback riding. The boys enjoyed the country. They especially cherished their times at Bal-moral and Highgrove, where they had protection from the press. Prince Charles also taught his sons about the British monarchy. He knew they needed to understand what was expected of them as members of the royal family.

Diana, on the other hand, thought it was important to show William and Harry what ordinary, nonroyal life was like. She took the boys to amusement parks, ski resorts, and vacations by the sea. She also taught them compassion and caring. "I want them to have an understanding of people's emotions, of people's insecurities, of people's distress, of their hopes and dreams," said Diana.

Once she took her sons to a homeless shelter in the middle of the night. "I want them to grow up knowing there are poor people as well as palaces," Diana explained. "I've taken the children to all sorts of areas where I'm not sure anyone of that age in this family has been before. And [now] they have a knowledge. They may never use it, but the seed is there, and I hope it will grow because knowledge is power."

Princes William and Harry at a theme park with their mother

Diana's work brought her in contact with people of all races and backgrounds. She loved all people the same, and she didn't hesitate to go places other people were afraid to go. For instance, she stunned the world when she visited a home for lepers in Chamba, India, and reached out to touch a man with leprosy. Diana helped raise $640,000 for the center and helped increase public awareness of the disease.

In 1990, Diana hosted a fund-raiser in Washington, D.C., for Grandma's House, a shelter for abandoned, abused, and HIV-positive children (children who have been infected with the AIDS virus). "Diana used her power just like a magic wand, waving it in all kinds of places where there was hurt," said Debbie Tate, co-founder of Grandma's House. "And everywhere she used it, there were changes—almost like a fairy tale." In a single evening, Diana raised more money for Grandma's House than the group usually collected in a year.

Often, her charity work took place behind the scenes, far away from the crush of reporters or cameras. Sometimes she would arrive unannounced at a London AIDS hospice and volunteer to serve lunch to the residents.

Meanwhile, Diana's personal life was not a happy one. She and the prince barely spoke to one another. Sometimes they had bitter fights, which their children overheard. Once after a fight, Diana cried alone in her room. Prince William tried to make her feel better. He stuffed tissues under the door for her.

Though their marital problems were serious, Diana and the Prince continued to appear together in public. In March 1992, Diana, Prince Charles, and their sons took a skiing holiday in Lech, Austria. While they were away, Diana received heartbreaking news. Her father, Earl Spencer, had died suddenly. The death of Earl Spencer created further bitterness between the couple. Diana wanted to fly back to England immediately and leave Charles to care for the boys, but Charles insisted that he accompany Diana. Diana felt that Charles was only concerned with his public image—what would the press think if Charles didn't accompany his grieving wife to her father's funeral? Eventually, the Queen intervened in the matter. Diana agreed to attend the funeral with Charles.

The tension between Diana and Charles had become impossible to hide.

Diana had also been unfaithful to Charles. In 1989, she had a love affair with a cavalry officer, James Hewitt. Diana and Charles couldn't continue their marriage any longer and planned to separate. Because she had been a child of divorce, Diana felt very sad. She knew how hard the separation would be for her own children.

In December 1992, Buckingham Palace officially announced that the Prince and Princess of Wales were separating. Soon after, Diana moved into an apartment at Kensington Palace. Her life as a royal had begun to change.

Diana knew that she would never become the queen of England. But she was certain of one thing. She wanted to continue working for charities and helping people in need. "I'd like to be a queen of people's hearts," she told an interviewer.

In January 1995, Diana flew to the United States on a goodwill mission—her first American visit without the prince. She was greeted warmly by thousands of Americans. Diana visited children at an AIDS ward at Harlem Hospital in New York City. She also attended an awards ceremony of the Council of Fashion Designers of America at Lincoln Center, a major event in the fashion industry.

Since reporters and cameras followed Diana everywhere, her popularity sometimes had advantages. She could use the never-ending media coverage to draw attention to the causes she believed in. Because of this, some critics called Diana "manipulative." They said she loved being the center of attention.

But friends knew how much Diana yearned for an ordinary life. "Everyone said she would go anywhere and do anything to have her picture taken, but as far as I could see the truth was completely different," said writer Richard Kay. "A good day for Diana was one where photographers did not pursue her and clamber over her car."

In 1996, Diana flew to southern Asia. She had seen a documentary about a cancer center in Pakistan, and she wanted to help. "There was a young boy who had a tumor on his face," remembered Imran Khan, founder of the center. "That tumor was festering. And she picked him up. She held him, completely oblivious to everything."

The hospital's medical director, Dr. G. M. Shah, also remembered Diana's visit. "She remembered [the boy's] case when she returned [in 1997] and asked for him," said Dr. Shah. "[The boy] had died shortly after her first visit. For a few moments after hearing this, she couldn't speak."

In June 1996, Diana traveled to Chicago to raise money for cancer research and other charities. She participated in a symposium on breast cancer and a forty-eight-hour fund-raiser to fight the disease. "She spoke eloquently about breast cancer," said Ann Lurie of the Lurie Cancer Center. "There was a sense of, 'she's done her homework.'"

While in Chicago, Diana toured the children's unit of Chicago's Cook County Hospital. Thirteen-year-old Alexandria Soriano, a trauma patient, was happy when Diana visited her in her hospital room. "Everything she had on matched, up and down," said Alexandria. "And when I hugged her, it felt good."

Altogether, Diana helped raise $1.4 million for Chicago charities. Some of the money was donated to Gilda's Club, a support group for cancer patients named after the late comic actress Gilda Radner.

Back home in August, with the queen's urging, Diana and Charles ended their fifteen-year marriage. In the divorce settlement, Diana received a payment of $26.5 million. She lost her title "Her Royal Highness," but she retained her status as Princess of Wales. Also in the settlement, Diana received a five-bedroom apartment in Kensington Palace and $600,000 a year to

Alexandria Soriano was very excited to meet the princess.

maintain her office staff. She and Charles would share custody of William and Harry.

Diana tried to explain the divorce to her sons. She gently told Wills about her husband's affair with Camilla Parker-Bowles. "There were three of us in this marriage," she said, "and the pressure of the media was another factor, so the two together were very difficult."

But Diana didn't want her sons to give up on love and marriage. She wanted them to believe that healthy relationships were possible and valuable. "If you find someone you love in life, you must hang on to it and look after it," she said to William. "If you [are] lucky enough to find someone who loves you, then [you] must protect it."

Diana wasn't sure if she would ever find love again. She feared that no one would put up with the reporters and photographers who followed her everywhere. "Who would have me, with all the baggage I come with?" she often asked friends.

A few months after her divorce was finalized, Diana saw an astrologer. The astrologer predicted that a new man would come into her life soon. She hoped the prediction was true. She was ready for happier times.

Diana called this benefit "Sequins Save Lives."

Chapter **TEN**

NEW DIRECTIONS

AFTER HER DIVORCE, **D**IANA HAD MIXED EMOTIONS. She felt sad, but she also had a wonderful sense of freedom. For the first time in years, she didn't have to stick to the rigid schedule and rules of her life as a royal. "I'd like to go to the opera or ballet or a film," said Diana. "It would be quite nice to go and do things like a weekend in Paris." Diana continued her charity work, but focused her energies, selecting just a handful of groups to actively support.

More than anything, Diana enjoyed being with William and Harry, who now divided their free time between their parents. Diana and Charles worked to get along with one another because they didn't want the tension between them to hurt their boys.

Sometimes, when Diana and Charles were out in public, Prince Harry made them hold hands. He hoped they would fall back in love, but Diana and the prince were past the point of reconciliation. Instead, they wanted to be friends.

Diana was much more comfortable in the company of sick and disadvantaged people than at glamorous social events. And she was tired of wearing evening gowns and diamond tiaras.

Prince William had a great idea for his mother. He suggested that she clean out her closet—for charity. Diana liked William's idea. She would auction off her designer evening gowns and donate the money she raised to people in need.

Diana contacted one of her godparents, who worked with Christie's, an auction house in New York City. Together they planned a fund-raiser that Diana jokingly referred to as "Sequins Save Lives." In June 1997, Christie's auctioned off 79 of Diana's evening gowns. The unique fund-raiser brought in $5.7 million for AIDS and cancer charities.

Diana's friend, actor Richard Attenborough, encouraged her to get involved in another cause—ridding the world of land mines. Attenborough told Diana that in many war-torn areas of the world, millions of land mines remained buried in the ground. Many innocent people were being killed or disabled when the mines exploded. Attenborough believed that Diana's presence in the campaign against land mines could make a big difference. Her international appeal could bring much needed attention to the issue.

Diana wanted to help. In January 1997, she joined the British Red Cross's campaign against land mines. She took an eleven-hour flight to Angola, an African nation littered with millions of mines. "No one expected Di to tackle this, to ditch the designer gowns and turn up in West Africa in jeans," said British Press Association reporter Peter Archer, who traveled with Diana on the trip.

In Angola, Diana worked long, hard days in unbearable heat. She toured hospitals in Luanda, Angola's capital. "It was at the hospitals, confronted with injuries so horrifying that it was hard not to turn one's

Diana learned more about land mines by visiting Angola with the Red Cross.

head away, that I saw something I'd never seen before: a completely instinctive sense of the right way to talk to the sick and needy," remembered Christina Lamb, a journalist who traveled with Diana. "There wasn't one victim whom she didn't leave with a smile on their lips or a new light in their eyes."

Diana insisted on touring the war-torn city of Cuíto, even though her advisers said the trip was much too dangerous. "It was infernally hot and dusty, and taking one wrong step could mean walking on a mine, yet she never complained," recalled Lamb.

Lamb remembers how, in Huambo, Angola, Diana continued to walk around a dusty, fly-ridden hospital—even after the photographers had left. "I watched her sit and hold the hand of Helena Uasova, a seven-year-old who'd . . . stepped on a mine while fetching water," said Lamb. "Afterwards the small girl asked me if she was an angel. I didn't have the heart to say no."

Diana posed for a photo with Sandra Txijica, a fourteen-year-old girl who lost a leg when she stepped on a mine. The photograph, printed in newspapers worldwide, brought instant attention to the problem of land mines. An Australian photographer named Peter Carrette saw the picture in a newspaper. He was so moved that he tracked the girl down in Africa and gave her a $1,000 artificial leg.

Diana felt happy. Her work was really making a difference. And the press was taking her seriously. With or without her royal title, she could make a huge impact.

Dodi Fayed

Diana's personal life was also looking up. In the summer of 1997, billionaire Mohamed al-Fayed invited Diana and her sons to vacation at his villa in Saint-Tropez in France. There, Diana was reintroduced to Mohamed's handsome son, Emad "Dodi" Fayed. Diana had met Dodi ten years earlier at a polo match in England, where the Harrods department store team was playing, and beating, Prince Charles's team.

The al-Fayed family owned eleven homes, Harrods department store in London, and the Ritz Hotel in Paris. Their wealth exceeded even the Queen of England's.

Diana and her sons had a relaxing vacation with the al-Fayeds, swimming and boating in the Mediterranean Sea. She and Dodi hit it off right away. Like Diana, forty-one-year-old Dodi had had a privileged but lonely childhood. He was also familiar with the pressures of publicity. The press called him an "international playboy" because he had dated many rich and famous women, including actor Brooke Shields.

A few weeks after the trip, Dodi invited Diana back to Saint-Tropez—alone. Their friendship had quickly turned into romance.

As expected, the press was curious about Diana's new relationship. Using speedboats and helicopters, the "paparazzi"—aggressive freelance photographers—followed the couple as they sailed on Dodi's 190-foot yacht. (A single photo of the couple could bring a photographer thousands of dollars from a newspaper.) One photo, of Diana and Dodi kissing aboard the yacht, appeared in tabloid newspapers on three continents. Journalists wrote that Dodi was Diana's first serious boyfriend since her divorce.

After the trip, Diana returned to her land mine work. In August, she visited mine victims and their families in Bosnia. She also visited Washington, D.C., where she encouraged countries to clear populated areas of land mines. She strongly urged governments to stop producing or using new land mines.

The press commended Diana's work on behalf of land mine victims. Back in England, Prince Charles and the queen also praised her efforts. But a few government officials criticized Diana, calling her a "loose cannon," and said she was meddling in things she didn't understand. "What is there to understand when people are having their legs blown off?" replied Diana.

Diana's work in Angola and Bosnia helped bring global awareness to the land mine issue. She helped raise $1.6 million and paved the way for a treaty against land mines signed by more than 120 nations in Ottawa, Canada. Diana was at the height of her personal and professional achievements. She planned to build new hospices, and Dodi's father had agreed to finance a charity for victims of land mines.

Late in August, Diana spent time with Dodi in Paris—their fourth romantic getaway since meeting two months earlier. Diana's dream of a weekend in Paris had come true—and more. She and Dodi also planned to spend ten days alone, cruising the French Riviera on Dodi's yacht.

Diana told her friends how happy she was. Finally, she said, she had found someone who really loved her.

Dodi said he was in love with Diana.

Chapter ELEVEN

GOOD-BYE, ENGLAND'S ROSE

DIANA WAS HUNGRY. SHE TOOK A BITE OF HER dinner—sautéed sole and scrambled eggs with wild mushrooms and asparagus. The food was delicious, cooked by the chefs at l'Espadon, the restaurant in the Paris Ritz Hotel. It was about 10:30 P.M. on a Saturday night, August 30, 1997. Diana locked eyes with Dodi Fayed. They hoped to have a private meal and tried to ignore the stares of nearby diners.

Earlier, Diana and Dodi had attempted to eat at a Paris bistro, but the swarms of photographers waiting outside the restaurant had prompted a change in plans. Instead, they ate at the al-Fayed-owned Ritz, where the hotel's security staff was able to keep the photographers at a distance.

Before dinner, Diana had called her friend Richard Kay in London. She told him she was in love with Dodi and that soon she would be reunited with her sons, who had just spent a month with their father at the Balmoral estate in Scotland. Diana's vacation with Dodi was drawing to a close. The next day, she would fly back to London. She wouldn't see Dodi for a few weeks.

Dodi wanted the evening to be very special. He had planned a big surprise for Diana. He would give her a $200,000 emerald and diamond ring. Was it an engagement ring?

"He told me how much he was in love with the princess," said Albert Repossi, the Paris jeweler who made the ring. "He wanted to spend the rest of his life with her."

In the past few weeks, Diana had also given Dodi special gifts: a pair of gold cufflinks that had belonged to her father, a gold cigar clipper with the inscription, "WITH LOVE FROM DIANA."

Photographers continued to intrude on Diana and Dodi. At about 11:15 P.M. the restaurant's head waiter came to their table. He whispered that about thirty photographers were gathered outside the hotel. Diana and Dodi discussed what to do next. How could they get to Dodi's apartment without being chased by photographers?

They left the restaurant and returned to their suite in the hotel, where they made an escape plan: Two

decoy cars—Dodi's Mercedes and his Range Rover—
would leave the hotel first, both driven by his regular
drivers. Diana and Dodi would leave a few minutes
later, in a smaller, rented Mercedes with tinted windows. The Ritz staff called their head of security,
Henri Paul, to drive the rented car. Paul had gone
home three hours earlier. Within minutes, he was
back at the Ritz.

At about 12:20 A.M., Henri Paul drove the rented
Mercedes to the back door of the Ritz on a narrow
private street called Rue Cambon. A bodyguard,
Trevor Rees-Jones, sat next to Paul in the front seat.
Diana and Dodi climbed into the back. "I saw happiness in their faces," said a hotel guest who saw them
leave. "They were laughing."

Paul headed toward Dodi's townhouse about four
miles away. He passed the brightly lit fountains of the
Place de la Concorde and made a quick right turn
onto a road called Cours la Reine.

At first, Diana and Dodi thought they had fooled the
paparazzi. But a handful of photographers on motor-
bikes had been wise to their escape plan. By 12:35, a
motor scooter, a motorcycle, and at least one car were
in pursuit of Diana and Dodi's Mercedes.

Paul sped through a tunnel on the Cours la Reine,
then toward a second tunnel. Concrete pillars inside
the tunnel separated the westbound from the east-
bound traffic. Just as Paul swerved left to enter the
tunnel, he somehow lost control of the car. A loud

squeal echoed as the car scraped the right side of the tunnel, slid left and slammed into a concrete post, then ricocheted off the right wall.

Henri Paul was dead instantly. Dodi was also dead in the rear seat. Bodyguard Rees-Jones, the only passenger who was wearing a seat belt, was alive, though badly injured.

A French doctor, Frederic Mailliez, happened upon the terrible accident soon after it occurred. He found Diana unconscious, with severe internal injuries, but alive. Mailliez says that ten or fifteen photographers were also at the scene—cameras clicking away, flashbulbs flashing.

Prince Charles and Diana's sisters—Lady Sarah McCorquodale, left, and Lady Jane Fellowes, next to Prince Charles—leave the hospital where Diana had died only hours earlier.

An ambulance arrived within ten minutes, but it took almost an hour for emergency crews to free Diana from the wreckage. The car had been crushed like an accordian, and its roof had caved in.

Diana was rushed to Pitie Salpetriere Hospital, four miles away. By then, her heart had stopped. Doctors tried for more than two hours to restart it. Just before 4:00 A.M., doctors pronounced the Princess of Wales dead of cardiac arrest.

The circumstances surrounding the fatal crash are mysterious, and the finger of blame points to several sources. Some people blame the driver, Henri Paul. He was driving at an estimated eighty-five miles per hour, and tests revealed high levels of alcohol in his blood at the time of the crash.

Some people, including Dodi's father, believe the crash was caused on purpose—to keep the British princess, mother of the future king of England, from marrying an Egyptian. Several witnesses said they saw a "mystery car" cut in front of the Mercedes just before it spun out of control. But most people blame the crash on the aggressive photographers who chased the speeding car through the streets of Paris.

Soon after the accident, Prince Charles and the other royals received the terrible news. Charles was distraught. He woke his sons in the middle of the night to tell them their mother was gone. The next day he flew to France to bring Diana's body home. The boys stayed at Balmoral with their grandparents.

The royal family remained in seclusion at Balmoral in Scotland until Friday, the day before Diana's funeral. Some people misinterpreted their distance as coldness toward Diana. But later in the day, the Queen of England made a moving television broadcast. She wanted the people of Great Britain to know how much she cared about Diana.

Mourners flooded to the gates of Buckingham and Keningston Palaces and left thousands of bouquets in honor of Diana. On Friday, Prince Charles and his sons greeted crowds outside Kensington Palace. Prince William, age fifteen, and Prince Harry, age twelve, shook hands and thanked people who offered sympathy.

The next morning, on September 6, 1997, a bright sun shone over London. The streets were filled with hundreds of thousands of people. Many of them had camped out all night. The crowd was eerily silent. The mood was somber.

At 9:00 A.M., Diana's coffin was placed on a horse-drawn carriage at Kensington Palace. The casket was covered with a flag called the Queen's Royal Standard. Three bouquets of flowers—one from Diana's brother and one from each of her sons—rested on top. A card addressed to "Mummy," from Prince Harry, sat in front.

Diana's carriage was accompanied by the Welsh Guard, soldiers in tall bearskin hats and red jackets. Slowly, the coach proceeded through the streets of London to Westminster Abbey.

Prince Charles took Wills and Harry to see the many bouquets left at the palace gates in memory of Diana.

Thousands and thousands of mourners watched the procession in London. Millions said good-bye as the funeral was broadcast live via satellite worldwide. People on the streets cried openly as Diana's coffin passed by.

"Britons are not famous for showing their emotions," said royal biographer Tony Anthony Holden. "We're supposed to be this stiff upper lip, reserved people. But those millions . . . on the street . . . today are following Diana's lead, and it's a warmer, human country."

Diana's brother, Charles, gives the eulogy at her funeral.

Diana's funeral was as unique as she was. Pop star Elton John, a friend of Diana's, performed a special song at the funeral, a new version of his past hit *Candle in the Wind*, originally about Marilyn Monroe. John feared that he would break down while singing the song. But since Diana had been strong for him in the past, he wanted to be strong for her. The new song began with different lyrics: "Goodbye England's Rose."

Next, Diana's sisters read poetry, and Diana's brother, Charles, delivered the eulogy. He said, in part:

Diana was the very essence of compassion, of duty, of style, of beauty. All over the world she was a symbol of selfless humanity...a very British girl who transcended nationality. Someone with a natural nobility who was classless and who proved in the last year that she needed no royal title to continue to generate her particular brand of magic.

Her brother also spoke of Diana's anguish at being hounded and mistreated by reporters and photographers. "My own and only explanation is that genuine goodness is threatening to those at the opposite end of the moral spectrum," he said. "It is a point to remember that of all the ironies about Diana, perhaps the greatest was this—a girl given the name of the ancient goddess of hunting was, in the end, the most hunted person of the modern age."

Finally, Charles promised his sister that he and his family would protect William and Harry and would "continue the imaginative way in which you were steering these two exceptional young men so that their souls are not simply immersed by duty and tradition, but can sing openly as you planned."

Late in the day, Diana was buried in the shade of beech, oak, and willow trees on an island in a small lake on the Althorp estate. Her grave faces the sunrise, on the land where she spent much of her childhood.

EPILOGUE

Princess Diana didn't fear dying. In a way, her work with the critically ill had prepared her for death. "In her last year she spent a lot of time with people who were dying," says Andrew Morton. "And anybody knows—it's a very arduous and difficult job to sit with someone who's on that last journey—and she did it all the time. She had a great awareness of what death meant."

Two weeks after Diana was buried, Prince Charles officially thanked the public for its "heartfelt expressions of sympathy." He also praised the courage and dignity of his sons and said they were comforted by the hundreds of thousands of condolence cards they had received. Prince Charles added that he too would always mourn the loss of Diana.

Many people worried about Princes William and Harry—who were only teenagers. "I am sure they are going through a lot of pain and sadness," said friend Alexander Burrell, age twelve. "Your mum cares for you and looks after you. It's really sad for William and Harry that they won't have that. No one can replace her."

Diana's sisters keep in close touch with William and Harry. Prince Charles's side of the family watches over the boys too. School routines keep the boys busy. At Ludgrove, Prince Harry enjoyed sports and lots of friends. In fall 1998, Prince Harry joined his brother

Princes William, left, *and Harry,* right, *received Olympics jackets when they toured Canada with their father in 1998.*

at Eton in London. There, both boys live close to their grandparents.

On holidays and weekends, the boys stay with their father. "When the boys were with their mother [in London], they were hassled because of the paparazzi," said a friend of Diana's. "But with their father, they're on the royal estates, they're undisturbed, and they find that blissful."

In her last interview, Diana told the Paris newspaper *Le Monde,* "Nothing gives me more happiness than to try to aid the most vulnerable of this society. Whoever is in distress who calls me, I will come running."

Indeed, even in death, Diana continues to answer those distress calls. In late 1997, Elton John donated the first installment of royalties from the sale of *Candle in the Wind 1997*—$47 million—to the Diana Princess of Wales Memorial Fund. Also, several recording artists, including Paul McCartney, Sting, Celine Dion, and Tina Turner, came together to produce a top-selling CD, *Diana Princess of Wales Tribute*. All proceeds from the CD sales will go to the charities that Diana supported.

Grandma's House cofounder Joan McCarley summed up Diana's legacy as she was watching four boys play in a house bought in 1991 with funds raised by Diana: "She's gone but she's like the gift that keeps on giving. Her touch goes a long, long way."

SOURCES

1   BBC Worldwide ©, *Diana: The BBC Panorama Interview in Full*, November 20, 1995, n.pag.

7   Kantrowitz, Barbara, "The Woman We Loved," *Newsweek*, September 8, 1997, 43.

8   Morton, Andrew, *Diana: Her True Story* (New York: Simon & Schuster Inc., 1992), 18.

9   Campbell, Lady Colin, *Diana In Private: The Princess Nobody Knows* (Boston: G. K. Hall & Co., 1993), 9.

10–11 Davies, Nicholas, *Diana: A Princess and Her Troubled Marriage* (New York: Carol Publishing Group, 1992), 29.

11   Ibid., 29.

11   Campbell, Lady Colin, 29.

11   Morton, Andrew, *Diana: Her True Story*, 19.

14   Ibid., 26.

15   Ibid., 25.

16   Ibid., 27.

19   Ibid., 29.

20–21 Davies, Nicholas, 48.

21   Campbell, Lady Colin, 59.

21   Junor, Penny, *Diana: Princess of Wales*, (Boston: G. K. Hall & Co., 1984), 102.

24   Morton, Andrew, *Diana: Her True Story*, 15.

27   Chidley, Joe, "The Tabloid Princess," *Maclean's*, September 8, 1997, 34.

29   Campbell, Lady Colin, 87.

34   Davies, Nicholas, 57.

37   Junor, Penny, 184.

39   Morton, Andrew, *Diana: Her True Story*, 70, 71.

39   Ibid.

40   Ibid., 69.

40   Barry, Stephen P., *Royal Service* (New York: Macmillan, 1983), 190.

43   Chua-Eoan, Howard, "In Living Memory," *Time*, September 15, 1997, 66.

44   Morton, Andrew, *Diana: Her True Story*, 73.

44   Campbell, Lady Colin, 179.

44–45   Davies, Nicholas, 97.

45   Barry, Stephen P., 202.

45   Davies, Nicholas, 99.

46   Ibid., 105.

46   Kantrowitz, Barbara, 43.

47   Junor, Penny, 218.

47   Davies, Nicholas, 103.

53   "Royalty and Fashion," Questar Home Video, n.pag.

53   Martin, Ralph G., *Charles and Diana* (Boston: G. K. Hall & Co.), 277.

54   Ibid.

54   Ibid., 282.

54–55   Ibid.

58   BBC Worldwide, n.pag.

59   Ibid.

60   Ibid.

61   Morton, Andrew, "The Diana I Knew," *People Weekly*, September 15, 1997, 68.

61   Martin, Ralph G., 462.

62   Chua-Eoan, Howard, "In Living Memory," *Time*, September 15, 1997, 66.

63   "The Diana Tapes," *People Weekly*, October 20, 1997, 104.

63   BBC Worldwide, n.pag.

66   Kay, Richard, "My Talk With Diana the Day She Died," *McCall's*, December 1997, 40.

67   BBC Worldwide, n.pag.

68   Ibid.

68   Chua-Eoan, Howard, "In Living Memory," *Time*, September 15, 1997, 66.

68   Reagan, Nancy, "An American Favorite," *Newsweek*, September 15, 1997, 65.

69   "The Diana Tapes," *People Weekly*, October 20, 1997, 104.

69   Ibid.

69   Chua-Eoan, Howard, "Princess Diana," *Time*, December 29, 1997, 102.

69   "The Diana Tapes," *People Weekly*, October 20, 1997, 106.

70 Ibid., 104.

70 Ibid.

71 Chidley, Joe, "The Tabloid Princess," *Maclean's,*
      September 8, 1997. 34.

71 Ibid.

73–74 "The Diana Tapes," *People Weekly,* October 20, 1997,
      108.

74 Ibid.

74 Chua-Eoan, Howard, "In Living Memory," *Time,*
      September 15, 1997, 66.

75 Gleick, Elizabeth, "The Men Who Would Be King,"
      Time, September 15, 1997, 44.

75 Graham, Katharine, "A Friend's Last Goodbye,"
      Newsweek, September 15, 1997, 68.

75 BBC Worldwide, n.pag.

76 Hubbard, Kim, "Touched by Diana," *People Weekly,*
      February 2, 1998, 82.

78 BBC Worldwide, n.pag.

79 Kay, Richard, 44.

79 Chua-Eoan, Howard, "In Living Memory," *Time,*
      September 15, 1997, 66.

80 Hubbard, Kim, "Touched by Diana," *People Weekly,*
      February 2, 1998, 82.

80 Ibid.

81 BBC Worldwide, n.pag.

81 Chua-Eoan, Howard, "In Living Memory," *Time,*
      September 15, 1997, 73.

81 Kay, Richard, 44.

83 "The Diana Tapes," *People Weekly,* October 20, 1997, 108.

85 Hubbard, Kim, "Touched by Diana," *People Weekly,*
      February 2, 1997, 82.

85–86 Lamb, Christina, "Love Among the Land Mines," *New
      Statesman,* September 5, 1997, 9.

86 Ibid.

86 Ibid.

88 Kay, Richard, "My Talk With Diana the Day She Died,"
      McCalls, December 1997, 40.

92 "Who Shares the Blame," *Time,* September 15, 1997, 53.

93 Ibid., 52.

97   Morton, Andrew, "The Final Farewell," *ABC News Special Report,* September 6, 1997 (September 18, 1997), n.pag.

99   "Text of Earl Spencer's Eulogy for Diana," *People Online Daily,* September 18, 1997, <http://www.pathfinder.com/ people> n.pag.

100   Morton, Andrew, n.pag.

100   "Prince Charles, "Heart to Heart," *Maclean's,* September 29, 1997, 37.

100   Hubbard, Kim, "Missing Mummy," *People Weekly,* December 1, 1997, 134.

101   Ibid.

101–102   Green, Michelle, et. al. "Death of a Princess," *People Weekly,* September 15, 1997, 72.

102   Hubbard, Kim, "Touched by Diana," *People Weekly,* February 2, 1998, 82.

SELECTED BIBLIOGRAPHY

Adler, Jerry, and Donna Foote. "Growing Up Without Her." *Newsweek,* September 15, 1997, 50.

Alter, Jonathan. "Diana's Real Legacy." *Newsweek,* September 15, 1997, 59.

Barry, Stephen P. *Royal Service.* New York: Macmillan Publishing Company, 1983.

BBC Worldwide, *Diana: The BBC Panorama Interview in Full.* November 20, 1995.

Blumenfeld, Vorick. "The Big Day." *Life,* July 1981, 68.

Campbell, Lady Colin. *Diana in Private: the Princess Nobody Knows.* Boston: G.K. Hall & Company, 1993.

Chidley, Joe. "The Tabloid Princess: Diana Was More Complex Than Either Her Friends or Her Foes Acknowledged. *Maclean's,* September 8, 1997, 34.

Chua-Eoan, Howard. "In Living Memory." *Time,* September 15, 1997, 66.

"Diana's Legacy: Landmines." *The Economist,* September 6, 1997, 47.

Dimbleby, Jonathan. "A Chance for Charles." *Newsweek,*
    September 15, 1997, 54.

Fairley, Josephine. *Crown Princess: a Biography of Diana.* New
    York: St. Martin's Press, 1992.

Gleick, Elizabeth. "The Men Who Would Be King." *Time,*
    September 15, 1997, 44.

Honeycombe, Gordon. *The Year of the Princess.* Boston: Little,
    Brown, and Company, 1982.

Horyn, Cathy. "Diana Reborn." *Vanity Fair,* July 1997, 70.

James, Clive. *Fame in the 20th Century.* New York: Random
    House, 1993.

Kay, Richard. "My Talk with Diana the Day She Died." *McCall's,*
    December 1997, 40.

"Mission of Mercy." *People Weekly,* February 3, 1997, 76.

Morton, Andrew. *Diana: Her True Story.* New York: Simon and
    Schuster, 1997.

Oates, Joyce Carol. "The Love She Searched For." *Time,*
    September 15, 1997, 58.

"Prince Charles, Heart to Heart." *Maclean's,* September 29, 1997,
    37.

Tyrer, Nicola, and Thomson Prentice. "Wedding Bells Heard
    Around the World." *Saturday Evening Post,* May-June 1981,
    10.

INDEX

Photo Acknowledgments

AP/Wide World Photos, p. 2, 45, 55, 90, 97, 98; UPI/Corbis-Bettmann, p. 6, 12, 18; © Alpha/Globe Photos, Inc., p. 10, 35, 50, 52, 64, 75, 87, 101, 103; © Marco Diedde/Alpha/Globe Photos, Inc., p. 15; © Jim Bennett/Alpha/Globe Photos, Inc., p. 20, 61; © John Rigby/Alpha/Globe Photos, Inc., p. 22; © Dezo Hoffman/Rex Features USA, p. 25; Keystone/Sygma, p. 38; Photo Switzerland Tourism, p. 28; Express Newspapers/Archive Photos, p. 30, 42, 67; Mirror Syndication International, p. 56; © Dave Chancellor/Alpha/Globe Photos, Inc., p. 62, 85; P.A. News Ltd./Archive Photos, p. 72; Reuters/Corbis-Bettmann, p. 70, 77; Reuters/Sue Ogrocki/Archive Photos, p. 80; © Peter Aitchison/Alpha/Globe Photos, Inc., p. 82; © Finn/Alpha/Globe Photos, Inc., p. 94.

Front cover, AP/Wide World Photos.
Back cover, © Alpha/Globe Photos, Inc.

ABOUT THE AUTHOR

Katherine Krohn is the author of several biographies for young readers, including *Marilyn Monroe: Norma Jean's Dream, Elvis Presley: The King,* and *Rosie O'Donnell.* She lives in Eugene, Oregon, and is also a journalist and a fiction writer. Born the same year as Diana, Katherine has closely followed Diana's very public life. Like many people, Katherine feels a special connection to the Princess—who often mirrored the coming-of-age, hopes, and heartaches of those who admired her.